Freda's Signs

by Debbie O'Brien

illustrated by Victor Kennedy

PEARSON

Scott
Foresman

Editorial Offices: Glenview, Illinois • Parsippany, New Jersey • New York, New York
Sales Offices: Needham, Massachusetts • Duluth, Georgia • Glenview, Illinois
Coppell, Texas • Ontario, California • Mesa, Arizona

Every effort has been made to secure permission and provide appropriate credit for photographic material. The publisher deeply regrets any omission and pledges to correct errors called to its attention in subsequent editions.

Unless otherwise acknowledged, all photographs are the property of Scott Foresman, a division of Pearson Education.

Photo locators denoted as follows: Top (T), Center (C), Bottom (B), Left (L), Right (R), Background (Bkgd)

Illustrations by Victor Kennedy

ISBN: 0-328-13305-1

1 2 3 4 5 6 7 8 9 10 V0G1 14 13 12 11 10 09 08 07 06 05

The people of Midvale needed new signs around town. Who could do the job? Everyone was busy—except Freda.

Freda's problem was that she forgot everything. But Mayor Martin and the townspeople decided to give her a chance.

Mayor Martin gave Freda a list of the new signs to be made. "Follow this list carefully," he told her.

Freda was excited to be Midvale's signmaker. She knew it was an important job. When Freda got home, she put the list on her kitchen table.

Bus Stop
Keep Off
The Grass
No Parking

On the morning of the job, Freda woke up late. She rushed into town on her bike. When she got there, she realized she had forgotten to bring the mayor's list.

"Oh, well," sighed Freda. "I am sure I can remember all the words."

So Freda began to work. The first sign was at the bus stop. Freda wrote *Bug Stop.*

"Look," said an ant. "This sign says we must stop here."

So the ants stopped. Soon many bugs were lined up at the sign.

That was a problem for the townspeople.

"We cannot get near the bus stop because of all the bugs," some people complained.

"And now the buses don't know where to stop!" cried others.

Freda was already making the next sign. She posted it in the park. It said *Keep On The Grass.*

The townspeople read the sign. Soon, they were walking, running, and biking in the park, right on the grass!

The park ranger came running. She was waving her hands above her head. "Oh no!" she exclaimed in a loud voice. "Don't crush the grass! Stay on the paths."

"But the sign says to keep on the grass," the people responded. And they continued walking, running, and biking on the grass.

That afternoon Freda worked on another sign. It was near the Acme Watchdog School. Dogs were trained to bark there. Several dogs watched as Freda made the sign.

Freda finished the sign. She posted it in front of the school. It said *No Barking.*

The dogs were confused. They were also quiet.

"What's the idea? Why can't we bark?" one dog asked. "That's what we learned in school."

"Read the sign, my friend," answered another dog. "We have to obey it."

The people in cars were confused too. They parked everywhere. They caused a traffic jam.

The townspeople told Mayor Martin about the problems all over town.

"Do you have any idea who is to blame for all this?" the mayor asked.

"It's Freda," the townspeople told him. "Tell her to stop!"

Mayor Martin called Freda to his office. He asked, "Freda, did you use the list I gave you for the signs?"

Freda looked down. "No," she gulped. "I forgot to bring it with me."

Mayor Martin said gently, "I guess you learned your lesson."

"I sure did," said Freda. "I'll get the list. I'll fix all the signs."

The mayor said, "I knew you would do the right thing, Freda."

So Freda fixed all the signs. Soon the town of Midvale was back in order. Freda became the town's official signmaker.

And now she always reads the list before she even picks up her paintbrush.

Safety on the Streets

Before Garrett A. Morgan came along, busy streets were full of cars, bicycles, animal-drawn wagons, and pedestrians. They all shared the streets—without traffic lights! Accidents happened all the time.

Morgan decided to solve the problem. He invented a traffic signal. It signaled when to stop and go. It helped pedestrians to cross streets more safely. The modern traffic lights of today are based on Morgan's design.